LOVE AND AFFECTION

WAY TO BETTER FEELINGS

PRITHWIJIT CHATTERJEE

Copyright © Prithwijit Chatterjee
All Rights Reserved.

ISBN 978-1-68554-167-5

This book has been published with all efforts taken to make the material error-free after the consent of the author. However, the author and the publisher do not assume and hereby disclaim any liability to any party for any loss, damage, or disruption caused by errors or omissions, whether such errors or omissions result from negligence, accident, or any other cause.

While every effort has been made to avoid any mistake or omission, this publication is being sold on the condition and understanding that neither the author nor the publishers or printers would be liable in any manner to any person by reason of any mistake or omission in this publication or for any action taken or omitted to be taken or advice rendered or accepted on the basis of this work. For any defect in printing or binding the publishers will be liable only to replace the defective copy by another copy of this work then available.

*I dedicate this book for my mother for her
kindness and devotion of her family .*

Contents

FOREWORD

The thinking came to write the books when I saw various incidents occurred in our society which was not very well with the relationship in our society.Many relation breaks-up and many children ignored their parents. Even they don't reply to their parents. It is not a good sign of any society. I want everybody reads this book and they realize the importance of the real relationship among them.

Every parents loves their children.So, every children should love and respect their parents as well. And we must know about the love and affection because we we clearly know about the love and affection then we know about the relationship between the lovers ,between the parents and the son/ daughter,and among the friends.

So, I suggest please read the book and know the details about love and affection which always helps you to build a strong relationship mind .And also give me suggestion about the state of love and affection mind of yours. Please read and share me your idea and thinking in details.

PREFACE

The thinking came to write the books when I saw various incidents occurred in our society which was not very well with the relationship in our society.Many relation breaks-up and many children ignored their parents. Even they don't reply to their parents. It is not a good sign of any society. I want everybody reads this book and they realize the importance of the real relationship among them.

&

Every parents loves their children.So, every children should love and respect their parents as well. And we must know about the love and affection because we we clearly know about the love and affection then we know about the relationship between the lovers ,between the parents and the son/ daughter,and among the friends.

&

So, I suggest please read the book and know the details about love and affection which always helps you to build a strong relationship mind .And also give me suggestion about the state of

*love and affection mind of yours. Please read
and share me your idea and thinking in details.*

• x •

I
PART - 1

What is love ? And why people fall in love?.And why are some forms of love so lasting and others so fleeting?.Psychologists and the reseachers have proposed several differrent theories of love to explain how the love forms ?and how the love endures in the human mind.? Actuallly the Love is the basic human emotion of their mind and of their affection which comes from their emotional thinking of their mind. But when we go to understand this how and why it happens is not necessarily easy in this state.In fact,for a long time,many people suggested that love was simply something too primal,mysterious and the spiritual for science to ever fully understand.

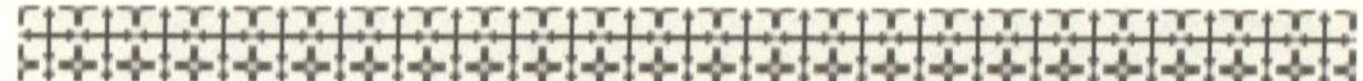

Thus the following major theories proposed to explain love and other emotional attachment of the human mindand the human thinking which belongs to the emotional human mind. At first we must know that about the linking and the loving of the human mind.According to the psychologist romantic love is made up of three elements,that are,- 1.Caring 2.Attachment 3.Intimacy At that time we believed that sometimes we experience a great amount of appreciation and the admirationfor others..We enjoy thatspending time with them and want to be around them. Butthis does not necessarily qualify as love.Instead of this it referred to this as yheir liking. Besides this we could feel the two types of love and the affection in our mind.

ಹಿ

That are the,- 1.Compassionate :Love 2.Passionate Love Now we must know about the Compassionate love and the Passionate love,then we could clear our thinking aboutv these types of love and affection of human mind. The love which you feeel for your partner during the early stages of the romance can feel much different than the love you may feel years later into the relationship. Actually the compassionate love is the feelings of mutual respect and the feelings of their mutual trust and their affection value while the Passionate love involves the intense feelings and the sexual attraction of each another.

ॐ

As anyone who has ever lived loved can confirm,not all types of love are the same.The love you feel for your partner during the all stages of your thinking .This is the real love and the real affection for your partner inn your mind. Actually the love affection characterized by the mutual engagement,and the mutual respect and the mutual care and the mutual trust and the mutual affection of each other in their mind While love is based on the passion which called the passionate love is characterized by the intense emotions,sextual attraction affection and the anxiety. But the affection usually grow out of feelings of mutual understanding and the mutual *feelings and the mutual respecting to each other.*

જી

But when love avenged which is the reciprocated love,where people feel excited and happy.but if love is not shortchanged which is the unreciprocated love which will lead to feeling sad and the desperate and even discouraged the life of thinking of human mind. As you feel excited when they are in front of a beautiful lady or a cool man.So,according to the psychologist the love Is a relationship that combines the comfprt and the love with passion itself. So,the relationship between the pair will last longer and the avoidable issue or the situation of divorce.

જી

Besides this the thinking of love defines into three parts of our thinking mind.They are as

follows,- 1.Realistic love 2.Practical love 3.Obsessive love 4.Conditional love 5.Unconditional love Besides this we could devided the love into three parts of our mind.These are the follwings,- 1.Passion –It covers between the romantic love and the sexual attraction of human mind. 2.Commitment- It is the decision to stay with them for a long time. 3.Intimacy-It includes the feelings of attachment and the closeness and the connectedness with them . We may define them with the combination of our feelings.that the combination of intimacy and the commitment is compassionate love while the combination of passion and the intimacy lead to the passionate love of human mind.

ॐ

There are the several theories which have not love attachment admininstration of the human mind.However,the some theories abou love most can not explain the love that have meen considered goods abstract abot the explanation of love and the affection. The three components of love which are intimacy ,passion and the commitment breaks down the diferent types of love and which components *are present in each other .*

Besides this infatuation is on the left because it involves only in the passion.It is basically the physical attraction aspect of their thinking. There is no emotional closeness invoved and an example would be a short relationshipsuch as if twopeople having a thing with each other. Actually the empty love is on the right because it has neitherpassion nor intimacy,but it does not have commitment to hold the relationship together. As for the two component of the love, there is romantic love which is intimacy and the passion. And the compassionate love is the combination of intimacy and the commitment of each other. And the last is the fatuous love which has passion and the commitment.

That type of love which falls under all three components isconsummate love. This basicallyis the ideal love that everyone wants to have their life. The significanceof the affection components are not lost on the marketers.The advertisement of the television and the magazine frequently depict a couples deep emotional relationship and their feelings of love ,affection and the intimacy of life. The family decision research has generally attempted to understand which family members influence one another in terms of family household purchases. Concerning intimacy ,It presents the three major components of love and other two arepassion and the commitment and it refers to the sharing that which inmost with others.

৪৩

It is clear to provide a more complete pictures of the family characteristics that definition and the functional values of the family willbe discussed from the affectional perspective. A comparison between the family and the other groups will be made to better isolate the differntiating characteristics of the family. Assuming that the affection is an important construct that influnces the family decisions.

We will explore how the construct fits and the definition and the functions of the family. The strong emotionalties in return may not be dissolved at the individual will and the unlike emotions and the relationships in other groups. Families are motivated to maintainthe intimate the emotional relationships by protecting the family and maintaining the harmony of the home which is intrinsic value.

&

But when we describe the love then at first we must describe the affection .So,Love and Affection are two inseparable feelings of mind. And Love is often described or defined as a deep affection where as affection is a feeling of liking and the fondness of our mind. However we will look at these feelings separately in order to examine the difference between love and the affection. The main difference between love and the affection is that love is the deeper and stronger than affection. If we love someone,we will feel affection for that person.

&

But we don't love everyone wefeel affection for. Love is always associated with the positive feelings like caring,warmth and the happiness. According to the ancient Greeks,there are foue types of love known as the 1. storge, 2. ,phileo, 3. eros, 4. agape Storge refers to love which we feel towards our family and the relations. Phileo refers tothe warmth affectionate, platonic love.This is the kind of love what we feeel towards our friends. Eros is a passionate love which is between lovers.And this is characterized by the desire and the longing. And the Agape refers topure love and the ideal love as opposed to eros.As these classifications suggests that love does not only refer to passionate or romantic love. It can refer to the love of parents,childrens,siblings, etc.

ॐ

Affection can be defined as a gentle feeling of fondness,caring or liking.It is a moderate feeling or emotion compared to love.Unlikelove,affection does not consist of passionate or rpomantic feelings. Yet,affection makes you feel safe and cared forAffectiopn can be seen in a relationship between a child and a mother,two friends,and wife and husband etc. In the simple words, when you love someone,you also feel affectionate towards that person..But affection is something you can also feel for those youdon't love.For example ,you may feel affection for your neighbour,but this does not mean that you love your neighbour.

ജ

Affection can be communicated through the gestures,words or touches.Huging, kiss on the forehead,cheek or nose are considered to be gestures of affection. Affection is the mild feeelings compared to love but love is the stronger and deeper than affection. Love and affection are the integral part of any intimate relationship.But sometime some people does not confess the truth of the real relationship of our life. So,unfortunately some adults today find themselves at a loss when seeking to nurture a relationship with that special someone.

ജ

Some have never experienced tender love and the affection themselves or have been hurt deeply in the past and now shun all forms of love and the affection as a defense against furthur infliction of pain. And the other think thatthey are being loving and affectionate only to find out too late that they have fallen short and their partners needs have been sorely unfulfilled. In order to understand that the role of the love and the affection in a healthy relationship and express them approprietely.

છ

It is important to understand that what love and affection are? Affection is the contact between the head and the heart.Affection is a deep long understanding commitment what your significant others needs are and the willingness to consistently strive to meet those needs. It is love in action and is the daily motivation to build a strong and lasting relationship with another human being.

Actually the affection produces the feelings of intimacy,security,significance and the respect in a relationship.Affection results in the tender feelings that are often called love.Iot is learned the behaviour and for many people,takes a considerable amount of effort to achieve.

ॐ

We are naturally born with yhe ability and the desire to love and affection takes a work. So, now the love and the affection have been covered and let's take a look at how to express them. Love is also considered to be a virtue which representing a human kindness and a good compasion and the good affection of the human life..As the unselfish loyal and benevolent concern for the good of another. It may also describes the compassionate love and the affectionate actions towards the other humans,one's self or animals.

ॐ

Love encompasses the range of strong and the positive emotional and the mental states of mind which is from the most sublime virtue or the good habit of the deepest interpersonal affection and to the simplest pleasure of life and the simplest pleasuer of the mankind of our society. An example of these range of meanings is that the love of mother differs from the love of a spouse which differs from the love of food. Most commonly that love rerfers to the feelings of a strong attraction and the strong emotional attachment of our thinking of life.

Love is its various forms acts as a major facilator of interpersonal relationships and owing to its central psychological importance which is one of the most common themes in the creative arts. Love has been postulated to be a function to keep the human beings together against the menances and to facilitate the continuation of the species. The word love which varies of the relation but distinct meanings in the different contexts. Many other languages use multiple words to express some of the differnt concepts that in english are denoted as love .

☙

One example of the plurality of Greek words for 'Love' Although the nature or essence of love is a subject of frequent debate,different aspects of the word can be clarified by determining what is not love. Love as a general expression of positive sentiment is commonly contrasted with hate . Asd a less sexual and more emotionally intimateform of romantic attachment. Love is commonly contrasted with lust.As an interpersonal relationship with romantic overtones. Love is sometimes contrasted with lust. Although the word love is so emotional and the exceptional attachment with our human mind.Emotional intimacy involves a perception of closeness to a another that allows sharing of personal feelings and accompanied by the expectations of understanding,affermation and the demonstration of caring.

ॐ

Emotional intimacy can be expressed in the verbal and the non verbal communication. The degree of comfort and the effectiveness and the mutual experience of closeness might indicate emotional intimacy between individual intimacy Actually the love creates the sympathy and the affection on the people who are involved in the state of love. Sympathy means the togetherness and the feelings which means the fellow feelings. It is the perception,understanding and the reaction to the disteress or need of another life form.

ॐ

This empathic concern is driven by a switch in viewpoint from a personal perspective to the perspective of another group or individual who is in need. Although sympathy is a well known term ,the implications of the sympathy found in the study of human behaviour are often less clear. Decision making,an integral part of the human behaviour which involves the weighing of cost with the potential outcomes. Research of the decision making has been devided into two mechanisms ofetn labeled the System -1 and the System - 2.These two system represents the gut and the head respectively,influence the decisions based on the context and the individual characteristics of the people involved. Sympathy ia an agent and the pathway of the System -1 and the system that uses an affective cues to dictate the decision where as system -2 is based on the the logic and the reason.

ॐ

The need for affection in human beings is unique in the sense that we are the social species who requires a certain degree of contact with the other human beings. Affection is more thanjust an emotion.It can be considered by some as a requirement in healthy relationships in the human mind within the human life also. A human without love is not a human being. To live without loving is merely existing. It is a robots life if there is no trace of love in their life . To be truely alive, to live, to feel, one must have someone to love. If love is given to one who can not accept it, then it burns even more painful than if there where no love to begin in its life also. So, always express your feelings and concerns the opposite feelings. When you are trying to explain to your partner that you need more affection, then try not to criticize them. And identity the love language which comes from them.

❦

Do not doubt your emotions. Remember to give and be affectionate too . Can a relationship survive without the affection?........Then the answer is that ,....If you can't be intimate with your partner, whether physically or emptionally or both, you cannot explain and expect to having a lasting relationship with your partner. Human beings require intimacy. This is why simple physical affections such as handholding, cuddling , hugs and kisses are important to your relationship.

If you arer upset about the lack of affection, then really you are longing to be desired. By ordering affection you may be noticed in your spouse a reluctance to be affectionate with you. Even if you are being affectionatetowards them,......affection may not be big on yheir list of their list of the ways they ways they feel loved.

ॐ

Think about the things you love and the write down your favorite characteristics about yourself.And the consider the aspects of your life you want to improve. And make a promise to yourself to focus on you and not everyone else. And the regain your confidence and it connect with others. Ask him about his thoughts and the feelings in their respectful manner. Every time when I chat with my friends,they tend to bring up how they wish their partner was more romantic and affectionate. They hate how their relationship has become a routine.They wish that their partners would take them out on dates more,surprise them with gifts,or tell them how much they mean to them. People often think that once you are in a relationship,... especially a long term one ,...... you don't really need to show how much you love that person,because that person should already know.When the person you are with doesnot feel attractive anymore,then things can go soutb really quickly. I spoke with the various person in my life about the affectoion and the love of human mind and their relationship.

❦

And from that conversation ,..I knew that how to get your partner to be more affectionate to ypou,.If you thats something that seems to be missing from your relationship. Don't be afraid to be a little playful with your significant other. By being cute with them,And it will bring back the happy memories of when you both first started to go out cutely touch their butt without them expecting it,and trickle them in bed,or make them lauggh by telling fun jokes. These little things will go a long way and will open the doors for your partner to be affectionate too.

❦

Romantic relationships are two way street.If you are hoping that your partner will be more loving and you have to put in the time to give them attention too. And from this situation you must talk with them and find out the top three ways of receiving loves are. Once they start to see how good this makes them feel.They will probably reiprocate that feeling back to you. You don't just want to do this to receive affection for yourself. But you do do want to make sure that this relationship is equal on both slides by showing how much you l;ove them and not just expecting affection only from them. When it comes to love ,It can be hard to maintain if you don't have the affection towards them then you must control himself and you must creates the affection in your mind also.

I repeatedly referred to love and the affection separately whenever I speak ,thats intentional,..... because love and affection are not the same thing. Love is biblical mandate and foundational to successful marriage. I am convinced every reasonably healthy person is

required to love and the others the way to the God designed..You choose to love someone else by putting their needs above your own.It is a commitment of your will. In marriage you feel the paasssion and the loving acts become person specific.Affection is also important between parent and child.An affectionate family makes achild feel close,safe and cared for as well. Affection must be an ingredient in all healthy personal relationships including those with friends and exdtended family.

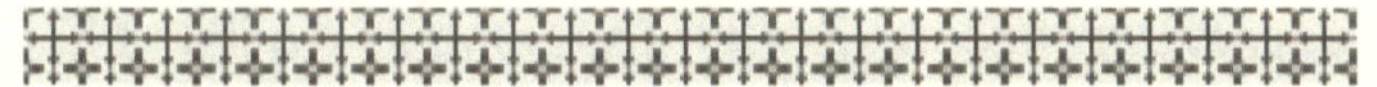

The Bible describes love in terms of action,not the feelings. Look at the familiar description of love from all the noticable of the actions required. I like to say though it may be grammaatically flawed that affection is love as actions that leave your spouse feeling really good about you and your marriage. Affection is one of the out working of love.Love is the commitment and the action and affection is the safe secure feelings that results.Strong marriages thrive when both the behaviour of love and the feelings of affection are present. This love as actions is what moves you the eighteen inches from your head to your heart.

Love is patient,love is kind and it does not envy,it does not boast.It is notproud,it is not rude,it is not self seeking.

ॐ

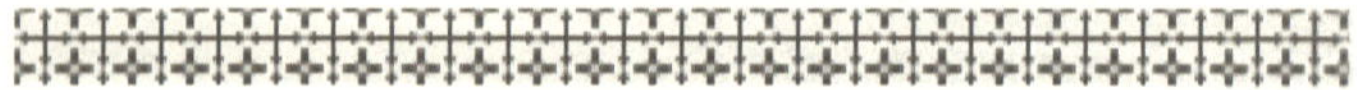

It is not angered and it keeps no record of wrongs. Love does not delight in evil but rejoices with their truth.It always protects and always trusts,always hopes always preserverence and the love never fails. This article comes from the book,starved for affection,written by Dr.Randy Carlson,published by various works of affection and love. Affection is the firststep towards love .Love is a combination of mental,emotional ,physical and spiritual mystic attachment to a person. Affection is when a person adores some one or something.Affection can be kept in heart for someoneor something while love speaks for itself.

ॐ

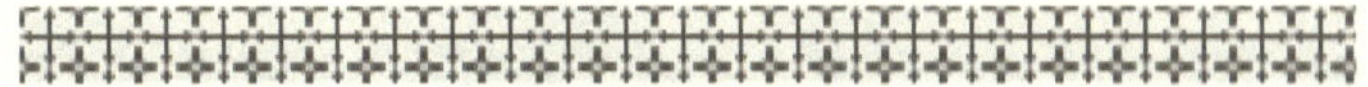

Affection can be one of the first things to go after children are born or when a marriage is in trouble. But it does not have to mean something serious and it can be naturally restored. Why after children the hundreds of couples have shared their affection and love what they used to give to each other time has been transferred to their children. Whilst this can easily happen,couples without children can go through periods of lack of affection too Affection of many people ,is what makes a relaationship a good relationship.If you are craving affection in your marriage right now and longing to be hugged,kissde or given the affection throughcaring words or the "I Love You "messages you are not alone. Thousands,if not millions, of couples may find themselves longing to be desired and cherished and its often because of bad advice that never ends and never works.

જી

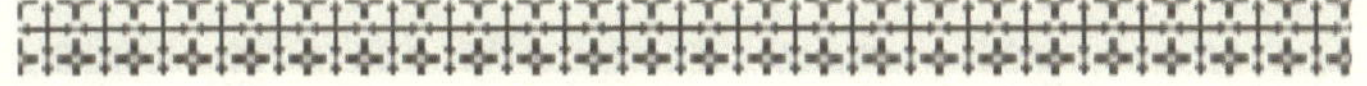

If you are upset the lack of affection in your marriage life then you may be feeling lonely ignored,unimportant and the unloved relationship. You may have started to see you husband or wife as distant,cold,self-centered,or only interested in the children. If this happening in your relationship right now,then read on as I will tell you what works and what does not when it comes to saving a marriage from a lack of affection and the lack of love . Talking about it, even just occationally ,will not get your husband or wife to change.Yet many relationship counselors may advise tellingyour spouse,"You are not being affectionate" It does not matter whether you beg,demand,or joke ,.It never ever works in the long-term or feel good to hear,for that matter.

&

Of course, your husband or wife may do not it when you told them to.But if you have ever asked for affection and been given it on demand, you know what I'm talking about when I say that it feels horrible.It used to make me feel more lonely when my boy friend hugged or kissed me because I presurred him to .You want your spouse to be affectionate towards you because they want to. It reminds me how I used to be around my Nan when I was young.She would always hold our face in her hands and demand kisses and cuddles when we wanted to just say " hi" and run to their back garden and play. Or when your mom wants to kiss ypou good –bye in front of your friends before school.It felt forced.

ॐ

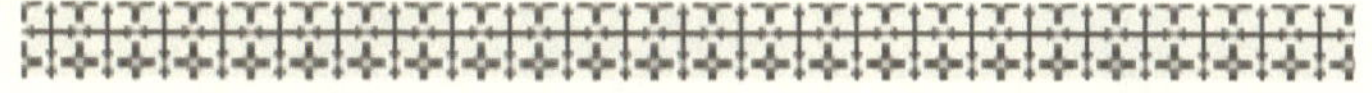

If you are upset abou t a lack of affection,ypu are really longing to be desired. By ordering affection ,you may notice that your spouces reluctance to be affectionate with you. And whenyou notice that ,it hurts eally hurts; I always used to ask myselfthe dreadful questions,-"What's wrong with me?"....."Why am I so needy for love and affection?".It harms you and makes your partner run further away.Stop listening to the advice that tells you to complain and instead,see their lack of affection as a sign that perhaps they are not feeling loved either. Even if you are being affectionate towards them,affection may not be big on their list of the ways they feel loved. Perhaps they need support in their areas where they want love shown in a different way

or are resisting control. Instead of telling them what to do or getting upset about something you cvan not control their behaviour and the practice making them happy and showing them love in different ways.

For example,through a,respect space thoughtful gestures or gifts. In a relationship,we can never control how someone acts as much as ew would like to.Controlling the behavior leads to distance,resistance and the shut down.Instead,if you focus on being happy,easy going and fun,the fliting,and affection will normally follow. Often when men or women confess to me that they know they have not been affectionate towards their spouse,its because they are stressed,dealing with a loss of some kind or concerned about the relationship or future. Rather than asking them to change supporrt them and aim to inspire them by being loving happy and full of energy and light yourself.

By becoming more focused on your own happiness and self care,you will become more attractive and can give them the space that they need. Bottom line fretting abou the lack of affection won't help you to save a marriage or make your marriage more affectionate.So,focus on what you can control you and watch the stress release from your both.Human are the social creatures. Some of us being more compared to others.And at the end of the day,we are all weired for engaging in social interactions with those around us. Sometimes an individual is content with just with their family members or a few select close friends.These needs very depending upon individual and their lifestyle,their experience,and their preference with their integrity.

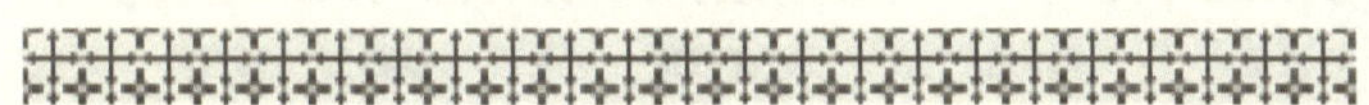

Sometimes a person needs to be surrounded by numerous friends and family members and

be in constant communication with others. Sometimes an individual is content with just their family members or few select close friends. These needs very depending upon the individual and their life style, experiences, and preferences. To go without some form of love and affection in our lives though can cause problems along the way especially if this lack of support and interaction begins at your younger age. Those who have gone without learning how to form proper social relationships and affection and who have impaired cognitive and emotional development as children often have difficulties. They have been found to exhibit antisocial and delinquent behaviours as children, teens, and even adults.

৪১

They will often show difficulty in the area of language development, intelligence levels and other social and cognitive skills. With support and treatment, many can overcome the instilled negative beliefs and responses stemming from their infant and child-aged years. The results are very depending upon all of the numerous factors at play in a person's life experiences that can span decades. At the core, though the lack of love and affection can cause potentially permanent and lifelong. Aging and becoming less healthy over the years is difficult enough as it is. When a man or woman loves them each other then their feelings attracts each other even mentally with physically.

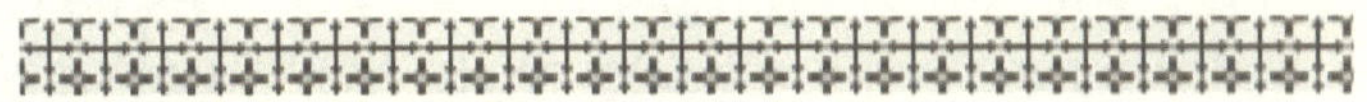

But besides this we observed that some men and women might not love his or her partner with their mind even their soul. Then the problems arise. If everybody will thought their mind with the another person's then they cannot betrayed themselves to their partner. So not only loves is important to the relations but also respect is necessary to all of this. Then a relation will be completed. When someone cheated their partner at that time it is not necessary that he or she understand this betraying. But whenever he or she understood the situation then he or she lost most of his or her loyalty and expectation from their partners mind. So, don't hurt those peoples who always loves you. Give them respect and love with your affection.

ॐ

Love and affection are difference from each other, but they are same in feelings and even they are same in thinking also. Affection is universal because affection may be varies among the son daughter and parents. The love between mother and son with her daughter and son is called the affection. Besides this the love between father and daughter with his son is called the affection. So, affection is universal and love is not an universal because love depends on the state of mind. And besides this love creates the place with or without the state of mind. Love could be affection but affection could not be affection because love and affection is not the same state of mind. Love and affection are two inseparable feelings.

ॐ

Love is often described or defined as a deep affection whereas affection is a feeling of liking and fondness. However, we will look at these feelings separately in order to examine the difference between love and affection. These main difference between love and affection is that love is deeper and stronger than affection. If we love someone, we will feel affection for the person but we don't love everyone we feel affection for. Because love is always associated with positive feelings like caring, warmth, and the happiness of those people. We know that according to Greeks there are four types of love that is known as storge, phileo, eros and agape. Stoge refers to the love which we feel towards family and the relations.

୫

Phileo means to the warm affection and platonic love which is the kind of love that we feel towards the friends circle. Eros is a passionate love which is between lovers. This is the characterized by desire and longing. Agape refers to pure and ideal love, as opposed to eros. As these classification suggest, love does not only refer to passionate or romantic love. It can refer to the love for parents, siblings, parents, children, etc. Love is a complex emotion since it consists of a wide variety of feelings, and states the love we feel towards a person differs. According to the familiarity and relationship with that person. Love for a child is tinged with other emotions like desire, warmth, attraction and affection. Affection can be defined as a gentle feeling of fondness, caring or liking. It is a moderate feeling or emotion compared to love. Unlike love, affection does not consists of passionate or romantic love and feelings.

ॐ

But affection is something you can also feel for those you don't love. For example, you may feel affection for your neighbour but this does not mean that you love your neighbour. Affection can be communicated through gestures words or touches. Hugging, kiss, on the forehead, cheek, or nose are considered to be gestures of affection. Those who have gone without learning how to form proper social relationships and who have impaired cognitive and emotional development as children often have difficulties. They have been fond to exhibit antisocial and delinquent behaviours as a children, teens, even adults. They will often show difficulties in this area of language development, intelligence levels, and other social and cognitive skills.

૪૭

With support and treatment many can overcome the instilled negative beliefs and responses stemming from their infant and child aged years. The result vary depending upon all of the numerous factors at play in a person's life experiences that can span decades. At the core, though the lack of love and affection can cause potentially permanent life-long damage. When someone is a part of a life for the long time,--- be a partner, parents, child or a friend,---it is all too easy to take the relationship for granted. It seems like a given that they are always going to be around no matter what? You get wrapped up in the minutes of everyday life, at home, work, and school, neglecting o show your love and affection to those who deserve it most.

૪૭

But with a little help from flo, you can make a change for a better. Regardless of your age, gender, sexuality or physical and mental *health, you – and everyone around you needs love and affection. So, why receiving love is important? There is a reason receiving love and affection feels so good. It is a phenomenon which happens at the chemical level with the release of oxytocin or the love hormone. Affectionate behaviours such as holding hands, hugging or having sex elevate yours levels of oxytocin. This is a turn, encourages bonding reduces pain and creates an overall calming sensation. Feelings of love and affection even appear to carry with the numerous health benefits by lowering your blood pressure stabilizing your mood and much more.*

❧

The mental emotional and social advantages of receiving love and affection speak for themselves. Aside from helping you to maintain positive and long-lasting relationships, Your confidence and self-esteem get a major boost. You and your loved one can strengthen your bond and build greater trust on you and yours also. Giving love is every bit as critical as receiving it in our quest for happiness. Think about how wonderful it feels to be shown and told that you are loved. And your partner deserves to experience that too. Expressing your love and affection motivates them to continue doing the same for you. What better way is there to demonstrate your commitment dedication and loyalty? Loving others also allows you to open yourself up to another person and discover your inner capacity for pure and unconditional love. Giving love is not about grand showy gestures.

≔

It does not take a lot of time, effort or money to offer love and affection. Quite the opposite in fact its actually a slow and steady process that's move about consistency and dependability rather than the occasional over the top display. Here are few pieces of advice on how to show love and affection to others. Don't do anything that does not come naturally to you. Not to say that you will never have to step outside your comfort zone. But when you do it, it should be to show the love and affection in a way that feels right for you and your partner. Don't copy everything to see in movies. On T.V. or hear about from friends. Consider having a conversation about languages of love or small gestures which make your partner feel appreciated. Once you understand how they prefer to be given love and affection. It will become second nature to you. How we express affection is often heavily influenced by what we learnt growing up.

ॐ

If your family liked spending lots of quality time together, for instance, you might value the same things in a partner. If there was embarrassment at expressing feelings verbally or physically, this may continue into adulthood. But there are no real hard and fast rules,-- we may make a choice to do things differently in our adult relationships. In the end, we express affection the way we do because that's what makes the most sense to us. If you and your partner are speaking different love languages without realising it, that is when there can be room for miscommunication and dissatisfaction. You might both end up feeling like the other does not say or do anything to show they care. And may end up wondering whether they care at all.

ॐ

For instance, if someone really values kind acts, but their partner's way of expressing love is, say, buying gifts, they may feel like they are not having their needs met. Likewise, their partner may feel the bunch of flowers they bought the other day was really nice way of showing they care, but was put out by their partner's underwhelmed reaction. Overtime, this kind of miscommunication can really drive a wedge in a relationship. Both partners may start to feel they are doing all they can, but that is still not enough to make each other happy. As a result, they can start to feel bitter and resentful. For a relationship to be healthy you both need to understand each other's needs. Besides this you and your partner may need to explore how to you both feel most comfortable expressing and receiving the affection.

৪১

If you think you might find this conversation difficult, you might like to think about the following. Don't try to talk when one of you is busy, tired or getting ready to go out, Set aside a time when you will be able to chat uninterrupted. It can also be a good idea to choose nice, comfortable surroundings in the living room with a cup of tea, for instance. You might like to use lots of "I" language, "I" sometimes feel, "I" don't always know how to "I" rather than "you" language. You often make me feel "I". You never seem to "I" this way, you are taking responsibility for your emotions and your partner is less likely to feel like they are being accused of things. Sometimes, it can help to begin by focussing on what you like about the relationship.

I love that we can rely on each other for the big stuff, but I was hoping we could talk about some day to day things. This can get things off to a more positive start and help you partner understand you are not just trying to get at them. For lots of couples, discovering that they are their partner are speaking different love languages is a real light bulb moment. They might have been feeling miles apart, but suddenly realise they do love each other it's just that the messages haven't been getting through. If you think that you and your

partner could do with help talking about any of the above, Relationship Counselling can be great way having conversation that you might otherwise find difficult.

ॐ

Your counsellor will help keep things calm and constructive and everything you say is completely confidential. Love is one of the most important human emotions. And for every way we feel love, there is a word or phrase that tries to express it. We say tries because there is a reason. Love has inspired countless works of art from poetry to oil paintings to rap songs. Its really hard to describe. May be that's why we humble humans have come up with so much colourful language express the way we feel. Every culture or sub culture has its own loving expressions nicknames and codes.

ॐ

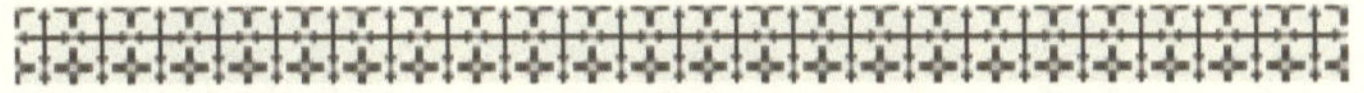

We have rounded up a few that we find particularly feeling and pleasing. Sometimes we love someone so much that it seems to be out of the world. That's where the expression of love depends on the mind of the person. One of the ways humans show affection besides buying flowers, giving foot rubs and making favourite meals is through the classic hugs and kisses. In fact these actions are so common that hugs and kisses has become a phrase to express affection in its own right. The two words have been paired as a set phrase for affection since at least the love with the least. When the expression often literally signifies the love sight between family members or romantic partners hugs and kisses became common enough to stand in for fond and compassionate feelings in general. This may be due to the fact that hugs and kisses is a familiar sign-off seen in the signature of a birth day Card from a grandmother to a good bye said by a parent on the phone. When this practice emerged is not exactly clear.

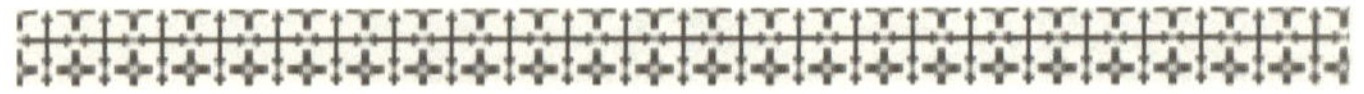

But it is surely influenced by the symbolic shorthand and its variant of love and

affection.143 is code for I Love you , especially used on pagers back in the 1990s. The shorthand as the story goes, dates back to the early 1900s from Minot's Ledge, light house off the coast. I repeatedly referred to love and affection separately whenever I speak. That's intentional because love and affection are not the same things. Affection is a fondness and it is a disposition of the state of mind or body that is often associated with a feeling or type of love. It has given the rise to a number of branches of philosophy and psychology concerning emotions, disease, influence, and the state of being.

&

And affection goodwill or friendship is popularly used to denote feeling or type of love, amounting to more than the open minded love and the affection. I repeatedly referred to love and affection separately whenever I speak that's international because love and affection are not the same thing. Love is a biblical mandate and is foundational to a successful marriage. I am convinced every reasonably healthy person is equipped to love others the way God designed. You choose to love someone else by putting their needs above your own. It is a commitment of your will. The love and affection words all refers to showing love or affection to someone or something. Affectionate is one of the most common words for this. It can be used to refer to physical signs of your love or affection. Such as a kiss or a hug. It can also be used when you described someone or something in away that shows you like a or love them. That is she was a affectio9nate child. T he word loving is often used to describe people who show their deep love for someone or something.

ॐ

Loving is not always used of physical affection but can be used to describe care and affection, or attention given to someone or something over a long period of time. Loving is used especially to describe the families or family relationships. He grew up a loving family environment. She was remembered as a loving wife including parents. The speech was loving tribute to his father. Caring is similar to loving. It is most often used to describe people who show their affection for someone or something by caring for them. You are a very caring person. He is kind and caring father, quite different from his own. If someone or *something is warm they show their affection or love by being very friendly warm is often used in the phrase a warm welcome.*

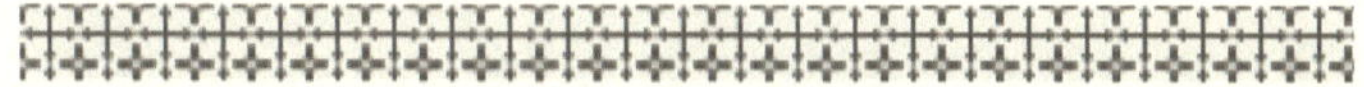

He had a warm smile. She grew up in warm and loving family. Lets a warm welcome to our guest in our house. But we know that the meaning of warm means hot and its opposite is the cold in the English literature. But someone is the warm-hearted person means generally kind and loving person to each and another. As a child he was very fond of warmhearted and kind-hearted. This warmhearted and the kind-hearted ness is the kiss on the cheek on their parents then it is called the affection of the love. And besides this the lover gave them warm-hearted and the kind-hearted kiss on their cheek to each other then it is called the love. Warm-hearted feelings can refer to actions that express a gentle and in affection for someone and something which is related with love and affection of this subject. So that this is more used when we only write than to express our feelings through the speech. Love and affection is necessary not only loving atmosphere in the

house but also necessary for your health also.

ജ

The need for affection in human beings is unique in the sense that we are a social species who requires a certain degree of contact with human beings. Although some individuals may be perceived as a loners maintaining the ability to ignore relationships with others there is still a sense of emptiness that exists when we are isolated from human interaction. Therefore, need for affection is carried across geographical and cultural boundaries and every country has their own special system of expressing their various emotions. Affection is more than that of emotions, it can be considered by some as a requirement in healthy relationships. Affection is an ebb and flow between two people, where each individual is giving and receiving a certain amount of contact and interaction at all times. Whether it is through a hug, kiss or just a phone call affection is the way we show others in our lives how important they are in the world.

ജ

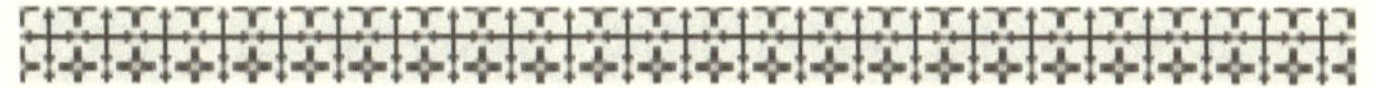

It can be easy to assume that affection is a type of emotion and when we mean that what is affection and why do feel the need for it in our relationships? Affection, much like emotions is a connection between two people, a kind of social interaction that can exists on varying levels. We can have a need for affection with just about anyone or anything. You feel affection for a family that is your mother and your father also. Besides this you feel also love with affection for your friend and your girlfriend and your wife also. You feel this affection for a romantic interest. What is so unique about our need for affection towards friends and romantic interest? What is so unique about our need for affection is that it can have varying degrees of intensities and depending on each of your specific relationships.

Affection and emotion is closely related to each other. But in really, they are different emotion is something attributed internally, while affection is something that you tend to give someone. According tobiopsychology.com, basically affection is work while emotion is something that just happens within you. When you begin a new relationship, you work at showing the other person how much you care about their well-being or about their happiness. You can fulfil someone needs for affection by purchasing gifts for them or by going to see their favourite movies also. This all takes work on your part to show that special someone just how much you care? Where as with emotions, we can experiencing this reaction throughout the day without ever having to physically show someone the affinity you have for him or her.

For example, just thinking about a person in your life can bring forth emotion and that particular individuals has no clue what is going through your head. Affection is also something that can be stored and saved for later events or moments in your life. We

provide the need for affection to others during various holidays, family gatherings or when a loved one is sick or dying. You may offer the need for affection to someone who is stuck in the hospital. Perhaps the holiday spirit provokes you to donate money to your favourite charity or give extra bonuses at the office. Whatever the action may be, you are not always bound to fulfill someone's need for affection every single day of your life.

இ

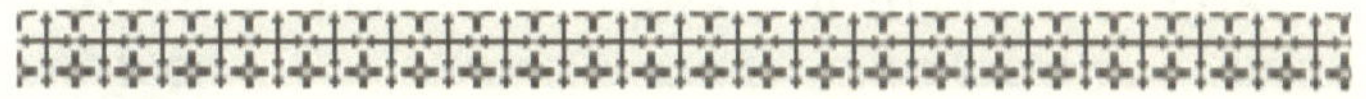

Why do we seem to have a need for affection, especially in our romantic relationships? The need for affection arises because it makes us feel secure and wanted by another individuals according to marriagebuilders.com. Parents wants to try fulfil their child's need for affection by helping them to grow into adults offering them advice when they encounter crises and providing a roof over their head. Your spouse fulfils a need for affection by showing you how much he or she needs you in their life. Affection is provisional glue that holds our different relationships together. The needs for affection solidifies our desire to know we are compatible with another human *being even if the relationship is on the friendship or familiar level. It creates a sense of harmony in a relationship especially when it is intimate one.*

According to the ones point giving and receiving affection means understanding our own emotional boundaries. It means understanding how far we are willingly to go out on a limb and put ourselves at risk for being hurt by someone. Fulfilling the need for affection requires us to let people into our minds and our hearts as a way to solidify a commitment . Love is a bibilical mandate and is foundational to successful marriage life including the successful family life. The healthy person in our society is equipped to love others the way God designed. You choose to love someone else by putting their needs above your own. It is a commitment of your will. We have known from the previous segment that love and affection is not same in manner. It is different in types. However the affection is step beyond the love. Affection takes the loving relationship[between a man and a woman in marriage into the deeper

realm of tender expressions.

It is one that results in feelings of closeness, passion, and security. Affection takes work because it requires knowledge of what makes the other person tick. You show affection when you perceive and appreciate what your spouse needs and meet those needs in a way he or she can understand. Affection results in martial contentment, intimacy, satisfaction, and anticipation. It is joy all wrapped into one package. Affection is not sexual. However, it naturally leads to sexual satisfaction. Affection is not a time, but it requires time to accomplish. Affection is not a direct communication. But without communication, there can be no affection. Besides this affection is not like a romance. But it typically involves romantic spontaneity creativity and fun. Moreover, when affection is present in your relationship, you just know it.

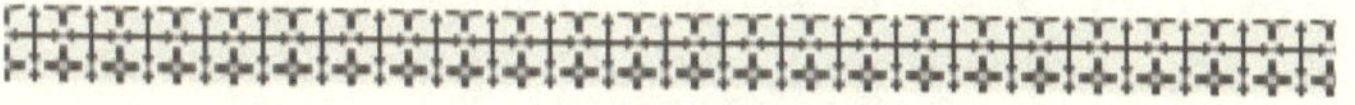

If you don't feel it, you probably don't have it. Here's my definition of affection. Affection is the kind of love that leaves you feeling close, safe, and cared for. In marriage , you feel the passion, and the loving acts become person specific. Affection is also important between parent and child. An affectionate family makes a child feel close, safe and cared for as well. Affection must be an integral part among all the family life and healthy relationships including those with friends and extended family. The Bible describes love in terms of action, not feelings. Look at the familiar description of love from the corner from the relationship.

Naturally love is patient and affection is the emphatic. Sometimes over-caring and affection can be a problem for an individual, because under such a situation, one often appears vulnureable and fragile. Afferction and love are the purest emotions that , now a days rarely few people have. People now

construe physical attraction as the epitome of love. Consequently, after some time, this temporary attachment declines between the two people and the reason is simply that they do not have pure love. They just have needs in some form or the other. Besides this it has been observed that it is not easy to find the right person with whom one can achieve compatibility. There always remains a certain difference between the two people and these differences later become a major impediment or source of a feud between them.

Conclusion

Thank you for reading this book. Hope the book helps you a lot. And it also helps you to gain the right path of your relatioship in your mind about your love and respect with the affection.

www.ingramcontent.com/pod-product-compliance
Lightning Source LLC
Chambersburg PA
CBHW051414250726
48655CB00003B/1043